TIM FOLEY

DOVER PUBLICATIONS, INC.
Mineola, New York

Bibliographical Note

2012 Political Circus Inaction Figures is a new work, first published by Dover Publications, Inc., in 2012.

International Standard Book Number
ISBN-13: 978-0-486-49041-0
ISBN-10: 0-486-49041-6

Manufactured in the United States by Courier Corporation
49041602
www.doverpublications.com

NOTE

The most prominent political figures of 2012 are all represented on the pages of this book of comic caricatures donning outfits that speak volumes about each pundit's reputation. You'll find David Axelrod dressed as a wizard and holding a crystal ball predicting the word "change," Joe Biden wearing a sporty "Not My Fault" T-shirt, Ron Paul showing off his "Emergency Eyebrow Kit," plus a hilarious host of others.

DAVID AXELROD, DEMOCRAT
Political Advisor to President Barack Obama

MICHELE BACHMANN, REPUBLICAN
Republican candidate for the 2012 Presidential nomination,
U.S. Representative for Minnesota's 6th congressional district

GLENN BECK
The Glenn Beck Program

JOE BIDEN, DEMOCRAT
47th Vice President of the United States, under President Barack Obama

WOLF BLITZER
The Situation Room

JOHN BOEHNER, REPUBLICAN
61st Speaker of the House of Representatives

DONNA BRAZILE
Political Analyst

HERMAN CAIN, REPUBLICAN
*Columnist, Business Executive, Former Republican candidate
for the 2012 presidential nomination*

ERIC CANTOR, REPUBLICAN
U.S. Representative for Virginia's 7th congressional district

JAMES CARVILLE
Political Consultant, Media Personality

STEPHEN COLBERT
The Colbert Report

CHRIS CHRISTIE, REPUBLICAN
55th Governor of New Jersey

BILL CLINTON, DEMOCRAT
42nd President of the United States

HILLARY CLINTON, DEMOCRAT
67th United States Secretary of State

ANDERSON COOPER
Anderson Cooper 360°

BILL DALEY, DEMOCRAT
Former White House Chief of Staff to President Barack Obama

MITCH DANIELS, REPUBLICAN
49th Governor of Indiana

TIM GEITHNER, INDEPENDENT
75th United States Secretary of the Treasury, under President Barack Obama

DAVID GERGEN
Senior Political Analyst for CNN

NEWT GINGRICH, REPUBLICAN
*58th Speaker of the House of Representatives, Republican
candidate for the 2012 Presidential nomination*

RUDY GIULIANI, REPUBLICAN
Former Mayor of New York City

DAVID GREGORY
Meet the Press

SEAN HANNITY
The Sean Hannity Show

MIKE HUCKABEE, REPUBLICAN
The Huckabee Report, Former Governor of Arkansas

JON HUNTSMAN, REPUBLICAN
16th Governor of Utah, Republican candidate for the
2012 Presidential nomination

GARY JOHNSON, REPUBLICAN
29th Governor of New Mexico, Republican candidate for the
2012 Presidential nomination

JOHN KING
CNN National Correspondent, John King USA

MATT LAUER
The Today Show

RUSH LIMBAUGH
The Rush Limbaugh Show

RACHEL MADDOW
The Rachel Maddow Show

IT'S AN HONOR JUST TO BE NOMINATED
INCORRECT

Bill Maher
Real Time with Bill Maher, Politically Incorrect

MARY MATALIN
Political Consultant

CHRIS MATTHEWS
Hardball with Chris Matthews,
The Chris Matthews Show

MITCH McCONNELL, REPUBLICAN
Senior United States Senator from Kentucky,
Republican Minority Leader

BARACK OBAMA, DEMOCRAT
44th President of the United States

MICHELLE OBAMA, DEMOCRAT
First Lady of the United States, married to President Barack Obama

KEITH OLBERMANN
Countdown with Keith Olbermann

BILL O'REILLY
The O'Reilly Factor

SARAH PALIN, REPUBLICAN
*9th Governor of Alaska; Republican Party nominee for
Vice President in the 2008 election*

LEON PANETTA, DEMOCRAT
23rd United States Secretary of Defense

RON PAUL, REPUBLICAN
U.S. Representative for Texas's 14th congressional district

TIM PAWLENTY, REPUBLICAN
39th Governor of Minnesota

NANCY PELOSI, DEMOCRAT
Minority Leader of the United States House of Representatives

RICK PERRY, REPUBLICAN
Republican candidate for the 2012 Presidential nomination,
47th Governor of Texas

HARRY REID, DEMOCRAT
Senior United States Senator from Nevada

Ed Rollins, Republican
Republican campaign advisor

MITT ROMNEY, REPUBLICAN
Republican candidate for the 2012 Presidential nomination, Former Governor of Massachusetts

RICK SANTORUM, REPUBLICAN

Republican candidate for the 2012 Presidential nomination, Former United States Senator from Pennsylvania, Fox News Contributor

GEORGE STEPHANOPOULOS
ABC News, Good Morning America

DONALD TRUMP, REPUBLICAN
Business Mogul

JON STEWART
The Daily Show

GRETA VAN SUSTEREN
On the Record w/ Greta Van Susteren